NUNCHAKU

NUNCHAKU
KARATE WEAPON OF SELF-DEFENSE
By Fumio Demura

OHARA PUBLICATIONS, INCORPORATED

SANTA CLARITA, CALIFORNIA

ACKNOWLEDGEMENTS

Many thanks to Mr. Dan Ivan for his assistance in making this book possible. My appreciation, also, to my most capable and patient young assistants, Douglas Ivan and Masaru Takenaka.

CAUTION: Use or possession of the Nunchaku is illegal in some States.

Forty-seventh printing 2002
ISBN 0-89750-006-7

PREFACE

Although the study of true karate encompasses many diverse facets, modern day karate is primarily considered self-defense without weapons. In centuries past, true karateka were actually warriors, knowledgeable in every means of defense and expert in the use of the weapons of their day.

It is my belief that all serious senior students should be familiar with the use of the weapons of these bygone days for the historical and moral enlightenment they can bring to them.

Weapons can be self-disciplining in practice, requiring dexterity that could not otherwise be achieved through normal training. With practice, the nunchaku becomes an extension of your hands. It develops a fluid movement—almost like kung-fu, a Chinese form of self-defense in which reactions flow smoothly from one step into another. In addition, practice with the nunchaku will affect your balance and help develop your wrists.

The nunchaku, of course, can be used today as a defensive weapon, but it is my lasting wish that no karateka who becomes skillful at the use of this weapon shall ever allow this knowledge to be misused or to fall into the hands of others who would misuse it.

FUMIO DEMURA

Los Angeles, California
November 1971

ABOUT THE AUTHOR

Fumio Demura, 5th-dan, was born in Yokohama, Japan. He began his martial arts training during his grammar school years when he studied the art of kendo as a means of building up his strength and improving his health. When his teacher moved from the area, Mr. Demura was relocated to another dojo which taught both karate and kendo. He then studied aikido in high school and, later, judo. While at Nihon University in Tokyo, from which he received a Bachelor of Science Degree in Economics, he developed interest in all the martial arts, including the techniques of such weapons as the bo, sai, tonfa, kama and nunchaku, which he perfected under the tutelage of Mr. Kenshin Taira and Mr. Ryusho Sakagami.

Noted in Japan as an outstanding karateka, Mr. Demura has been honored by martial artists and government officials alike. In 1961 he won the All-Japan Karate Free-Style Tournament and was lauded as one of Japan's top eight players for three consecutive years, from 1961-64. His tournament wins have been numerous, including the East Japan, Shito-Ryu Annual and Kanto District championships. He received the All-Japan Karate Federation President's trophy for outstanding tournament play and has received certificates of recognition from such Japanese Cabinet officials as the Ministers of Education, Finance and Transportation for his outstanding achievements in and contributions to the art of karate.

In response to an invitation by Mr. Dan Ivan, Fumio Demura came to the United States in 1965 to teach Shito-Ryu—one of the four major systems of karate in the world. He now heads his own dojo in Santa Ana, California and supervises instruction at the University of California at Irvine, Orange Coast College and Fullerton State College. In addition, he is the director of the Japan Karate Federation in the United States and advisor for the Pan-American Karate Association.

Besides his full-time job as an instructor, Mr. Demura has taken

on a strenuous demonstration schedule at Japanese Village and
Deer Park in Buena Park, California where his exhibitions have
become a very important part of the park's attractions.

In 1969 the Black Belt Magazine Hall of Fame paid tribute to
the author's dedication to karate with its coveted Karate Sensei of
the Year award. Mr. Demura's first book, *Shito-Ryu Karate*, was
published in 1971.

DEDICATION

The person initially responsible for my knowledge of and interest in kobudo, especially in the nunchaku, is the late Okinawan karate master Kenshin Taira. It was on one of my visits to Okinawa that Master Taira consented to take me under his wings and instruct me in weapons. Mr. Taira, who lived to be nearly 80 years of age, was a living legend—a perfect example of the gentle spirit of the martial arts.

Equally as motivating was one of Japan's foremost weapons experts, Ryusho Sakagami, who was my personal instructor in Japan.

CONTENTS

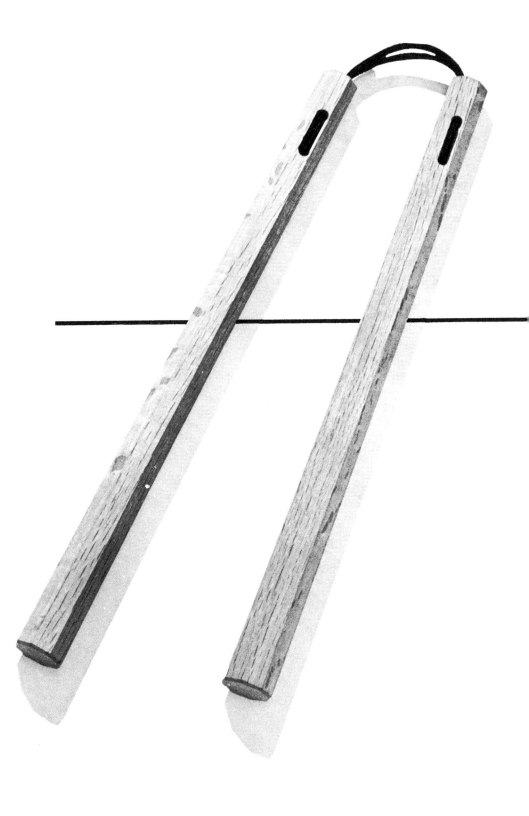

HISTORY OF THE NUNCHAKU

During the Japanese occupation of Okinawa some 350 years ago, invading warlords prohibited the use of ordinary weapons such as the gun, sword and spear. So, the Okinawans turned to karate and *kobu-do* (the use of karate weapons such as the *bo*, a staff; *sai*, a short sword with two prongs at the handle; *kama*, a sickle; and *surushin*, a length of rope with weights attached to both ends) for protection. Some kobu-do weapons were farm implements which the ingenious farmers converted into effective protective devices. For instance, the forerunner of the nunchaku was an instrument used as a bit for horses, and was later put to practical use as a weapon. The nunchaku was constructed of two hardwood sticks which were securely connected by rope braided from horses' tails. (Today, the sticks are tied with rope or chain.) Because of its innocent appearance, the nunchaku could easily be mistaken for a toy or harmless bundle of sticks. In a defensive situation, however, it could be used to strike, block, hit, twist and pinch.

The early practitioners of karate in Okinawa quickly incorporated the art of kobu-do because of its effectiveness, and today many movements of the two arts are alike. Therefore, it is very important that the nunchaku student also have a good knowledge of karate basics.

ANATOMY OF THE NUNCHAKU

Nunchaku handles should be made from a hardwood that, like oak, loquat or pasania, is both strong and flexible. The nunchaku rope, originally made of horsehair, is now usually made of nylon or chain.

The length of the nunchaku should normally equal the distance from the middle of the hand to the elbow. However, the size of the nunchaku should also be adjusted to fit the individual's height, weight and arm power.

Every part of the nunchaku is potentially useful. The bottoms and tops of the nunchaku handles are used to jab or spear; the upper and lower handle areas are used in swinging strikes; the middle area is for blocking and striking; and the rope serves to pinch or choke.

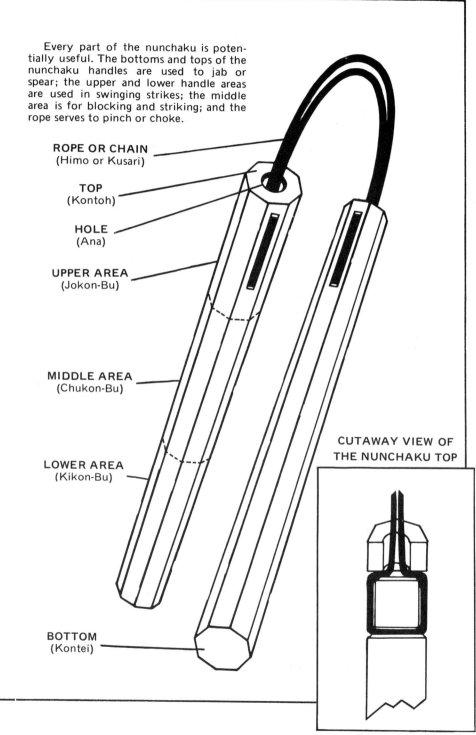

ROPE OR CHAIN
(Himo or Kusari)

TOP
(Kontoh)

HOLE
(Ana)

UPPER AREA
(Jokon-Bu)

MIDDLE AREA
(Chukon-Bu)

LOWER AREA
(Kikon-Bu)

BOTTOM
(Kontei)

CUTAWAY VIEW OF
THE NUNCHAKU TOP

CARE OF THE NUNCHAKU

CARE OF THE NUNCHAKU

The nunchaku should be cleaned once a month with a cloth moistened with olive oil, camellia oil or any other plant oil. This will make the nunchaku easier to grip and prevent slipping.

If the nylon rope is used, the inside edges of the nunchaku handles should be coated with candle wax to reduce wear. The rope itself may also be coated with wax.

TYPES OF NUNCHAKU

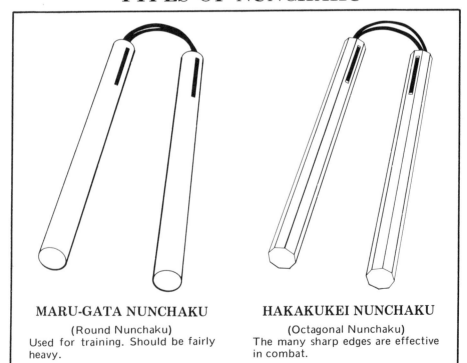

MARU-GATA NUNCHAKU
(Round Nunchaku)
Used for training. Should be fairly heavy.

HAKAKUKEI NUNCHAKU
(Octagonal Nunchaku)
The many sharp edges are effective in combat.

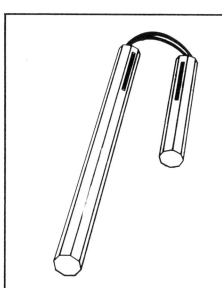

SO-SETSU-KON NUNCHAKU

(Long and Short Nunchaku)
One short side prevents striking your own hand during the whipping motion.

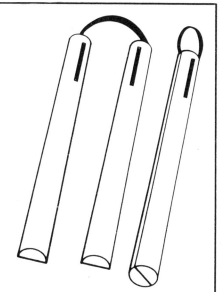

HAN-KEI NUNCHAKU

(Half-Size Nunchaku)
Two sides fit smoothly together, making this variation easy to carry.

SAN-SETSU-KON NUNCHAKU

(Three-Piece Nunchaku)
All pieces are of equal length. With all nunchaku constructed of more than two pieces, one of the pieces can be cut or torn off and the nunchaku will still be an effective weapon.

 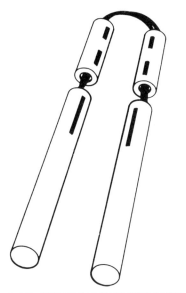

SAN-SETSU-KON NUNCHAKU

(Three-Piece Nunchaku)
One side is the usual length; but the opposite side is composed of two shorter pieces.

YON SETSU-KON NUNCHAKU

(Four-Piece Nunchaku)
Affords greatest attacking range and length sufficient to completely loop a weapon.

HOW TO GRIP
THE NUNCHAKU

Clutch the end of the nuncha-ku handle, locking and fold-ing your thumb over the fore-finger in a manner similar to a karate fist.

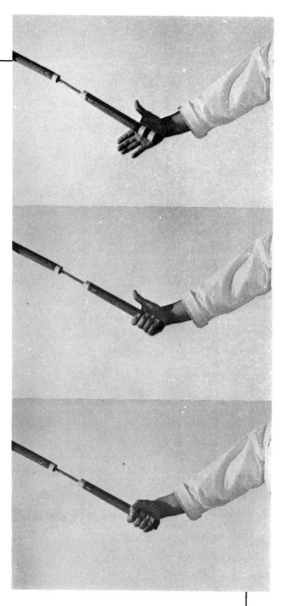

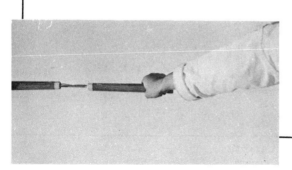

STANCES

Nunchaku stances are identical to karate stances. Stay well balanced and maintain proper hip position at all times.

**READY POSITION
(Yoi)**

All stances begin from the ready position.

BACK STANCE
(Kokutsu-Dachi)

The back stance is used to defend against a frontal attack. Put most of your weight on your rear leg so that it may be used for support.

FORWARD STANCE
(Zenkutsu-Dachi)

The forward stance is used to attack. Put most of your weight on your forward leg to propel your momentum forward into the attack.

CAT STANCE
(Nekoashi-Dachi)

The cat stance emphasizes maneuverability, allowing you to kick with your forward leg in combination with a nunchaku strike. Put most of your weight on your rear leg, leaving your forward leg flexible for attack.

REAR DEFENSE STANCE
(Gyaku-Zenkutsu-Dachi)

The rear defense stance is used to retreat from an attack from the rear. Weight distribution and foot positions are the same as in the forward stance.

CRANE STANCE
(Sagiashi-Dachi)

The crane stance is used to defend against footsweep or weapon attacks to your legs. Raise the leg being attacked and shift your body back out of range at the same time.

STRADDLE-LEG STANCE
(Hiko-Dachi)

The straddle-leg stance is used when you are backed against a wall by an attacker directly in front of you. Stand with your legs spread apart, knees bent and toes pointing outward so that you can move to either your left or right. Wrap the nunchaku around the back of your waist.

NATURAL STANCE
(T-Dachi)

The natural stance is used while awaiting an opponent's move. You can move forward, backward and to both sides from this stance. Keep the nunchaku over your shoulder.

GRASPING POSITIONS

The following grasping positions can be used from almost any stance.

DRAW AND STRIKE POSITION

The nunchaku is easily drawn with your right hand from under the belt on your left hip. If taken by surprise, you can draw and quickly strike in the same motion.

PARRY GRIP POSITION

The front hand grips the top of one of the nunchaku handles which is tilted outward in front of you to permit a striking maneuver, similar to a fencer's parry. The other handle is in a regular position.

READY POSITION

One handle of the nunchaku is gripped directly in front of you while the other handle is gripped in the left hand, ready to be snapped.

REAR HANGING POSITION

One handle of the nunchaku hangs over a shoulder, ready to be snapped overhand into a downward or circular attack.

DOUBLE GRIP POSITION

The nunchaku is grasped in the right hand, ready to parry.

READY POSITION

One handle of the nunchaku is gripped under the right armpit, ready to be released with a snap of the right hand.

VARIATION OF UPWARD BLOCK POSITION

The forward nunchaku, similar to an upward block, is tilted slightly inward with the right hand, ready to be released with either hand and whipped in either a circular or overhand pattern.

REVERSE UPWARD BLOCK POSITION

The upper (blocking) nunchaku is gripped tightly with the thumb at the end of the handle and is aligned with your right forearm, prepared to defend against attacks to the head or upper body.

CIRCULAR READY POSITION

One handle of the nunchaku is stretched with the left hand behind your back while the right·hand holds the front handle, ready to attack with a wide, circular swing from the forward stance.

REAR READY POSITION

The nunchaku is wrapped around the back at the waist, ready to attack from either side.

BLOCKING

Timing is of primary importance in blocking techniques. You must time your block with the attack so that it is neither too fast nor too slow. Also, you must calculate the distance of the attack.

DOWNWARD WHIP BLOCK
Against a bo attack to the leg, swing the nunchaku down sharply to parry the bo.

DOUBLE DOWN BLOCK
Against a kick or an underhand punch to the midsection, block the blow by jamming both nunchaku handles downward into the attacking force.

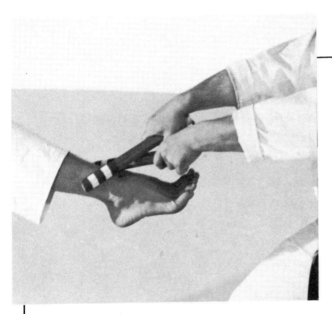

LOWER CROSS BLOCK
Against a front kick to the midsection, jam the attacking force with a nunchaku cross block.

DOWNWARD STRIKE DOUBLE BLOCK
Against a low kick or weapon attack to the leg, parry with both nunchaku handles gripped in one hand.

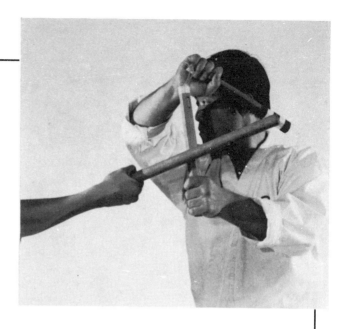

SIDE BLOCK
Against a roundhouse punch or a weapon side attack, raise the nunchaku to protect your head.

DEFLECTING BLOCK WITH ROPE
Against a lunging punch, a high kick or a weapon thrust, deflect the attack with the nunchaku rope.

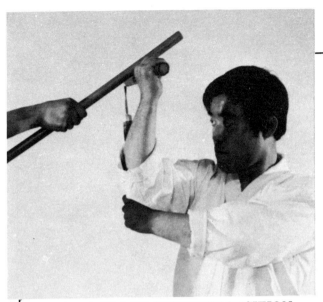

UPWARD BLOCK, REVERSE POSITION

Against a weapon attack from above, use the nunchaku to block the blow. Note: Because an overhead blow is powerful, you have to grasp the nunchaku firmly with your right hand and brace your elbow with your left hand.

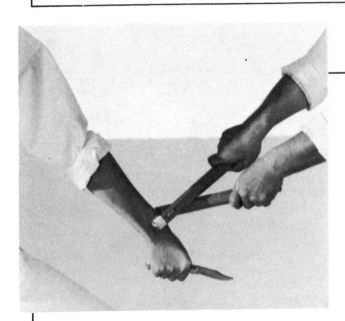

TOP SIDE CROSS BLOCK

Against an underhand attack or low kick, use a nunchaku cross block.

STRIKING

Most striking movements are executed with a powerful snapping movement from the wrist. Keep in mind the size of your nunchaku and the distance from your opponent.

BOTTOM THRUST

The nunchaku can be used to jam the handle end into the opponent's solar plexus or other vulnerable areas.

DOUBLE THRUST DOWNWARD
Drive both nunchaku handles into the back of the opponent's head or neck.

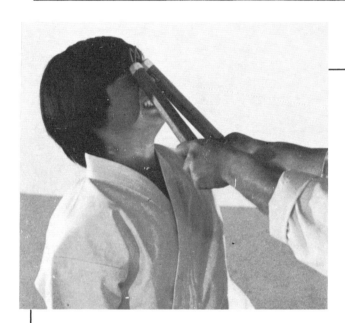

DOUBLE SPEARING
Spear the opponent's face with the top ends of both nunchaku handles.

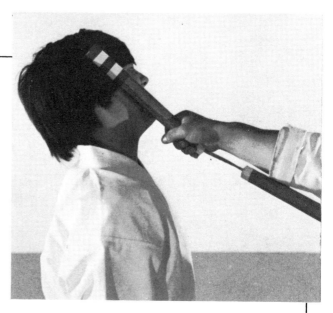

DOWNWARD BOTTOM STRIKE
Club the nunchaku into the side of the opponent's face.

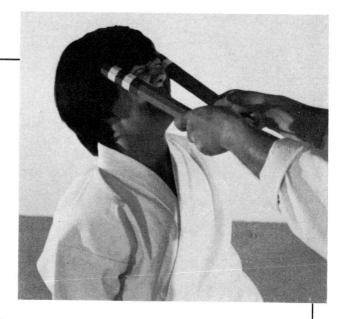

DOUBLE STRIKE
Strike the opponent's face with the bottom ends of both nunchaku handles.

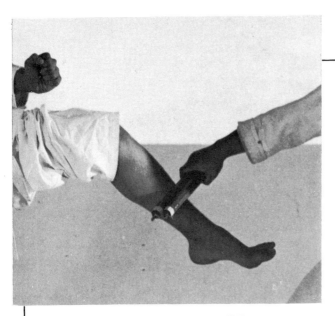

DOUBLE DOWNWARD STRIKE
Strike downward to the shin or other vulnerable area with both nunchaku handles gripped in one hand.

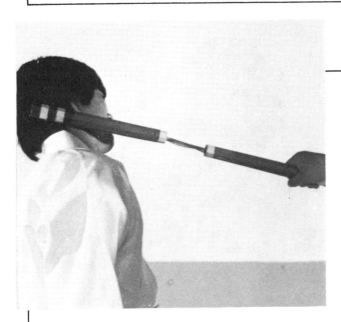

SWINGING BOTTOM STRIKE
Swing the nunchaku into the side of the opponent's head or other vulnerable area.

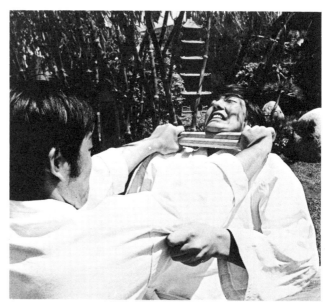

CHOKING

In most choking techniques the rope between the two sides of the nunchaku is used. The shorter rope will be more powerful. Timing the speed and distance of the attack is also important in this defense.

REAR BAR

From behind, bar both nunchaku handles under the opponent's chin and pull firmly.

REAR SCISSORS
Loop the nunchaku rope over your opponent's face, then squeeze the handles.

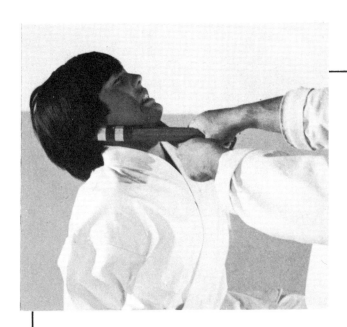

FRONT CHOKE
Use the bottom ends of a crossed nunchaku to choke the opponent.

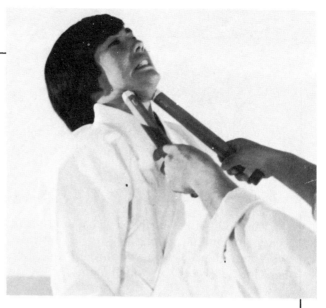

ROPE JAM
Jam the nunchaku rope into the opponent's throat.

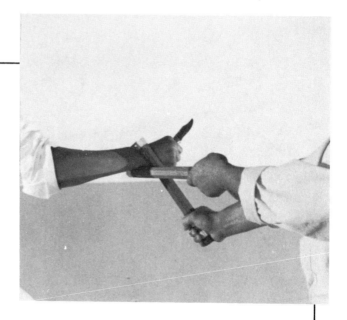

PINCHING
Loop the rope around the opponent's wrist and squeeze the nunchaku handles.

WARM-UP CALISTHENICS

The following warm-up calisthenics should be done before every nunchaku training session to improve your finger control, wrist and elbow action, weight shifting, shoulder and hip twisting and footwork—all of which combine to give the nunchaku its power.

In the early stages of nunchaku training, the beginner should concentrate on striking, blocking and gripping techniques.

To limber up your wrists, grasp both nunchaku handles in one hand in front of you and rotate your wrist.

To condition your spine, hold the nunchaku overhead and make deep twists from side to side.

To limber up your waist, hold the nunchaku in front of you and twist from side to side.

To limber up your legs and waist, loop the nunchaku rope around your foot and touch your forehead to your knee.

46

MOVEMENTS

As you begin to combine basic footwork with the nunchaku strikes and blocks, place the emphasis on fluidity and variety. Practice the following movements shuffling both forward and backward, and make the individual movements flow into each other.

BASIC ONE-HAND MOVEMENTS

From the (1) ready position, (2) grip both handles of the nunchaku and raise it overhead. (3) Then step forward and (4) strike downward. (5) Return to the ready position.

1

2

3

4

5

BASIC TWO-HAND MOVEMENTS

From the (1) ready position with the nunchaku in front of you, (2) twist your arms inward so that the rope end points toward you. (4) Then raise the nunchaku overhead and step forward before (5) striking downward.

1

2

3

4

5

DUAL STRIKE

From a (1) parrying position, (2) lean back on your rear (supporting) leg
and (3) swing the nunchaku counterclockwise overhead, then (4)

downward into the (5) outward strike. (6) Then withdraw the striking handle by passing your left ear and (7-8) snap into a backhand strike.

DUAL BLOCK

From the (1) ready position, (2) raise the nunchaku in front of you. (3-4) As you step forward place your right arm upright so that your arm and the nunchaku form a square to protect your upper body. (5-7) Then advance with your left foot and change grips so that (8) your right hand is gripping the vertical handle and the square is protecting your left side. Side view below.

SIDE VIEW

KARATE AND NUNCHAKU SIMILARITIES

Any karate movement may be used with the nunchaku if you consider the nunchaku an extension of that movement. During practice, remember good karate form for distance, balance and footwork.

UPWARD BLOCK

Without a weapon, a forward lunge punch to the face is countered with an upward block. Against a *bo* (staff), the defender holds the blocking nunchaku tightly underneath his right forearm to perform the same block. Front view at right.

CROSS BLOCK

Without a weapon, a forward lunge punch to the face is countered with a cross block—hands either open or closed. Against a bo, the defender uses the nunchaku cross block. Front view at left.

DOWNWARD BLOCK

Without a weapon, a low punch to the stomach region is countered with a downward block. Against a bo thrust to the midsection or groin, the defender uses the nunchaku to parry the blow. This block is also used against kicks. Front view at right.

KNIFE-HAND BLOCK

Without a weapon, a punch to the chest is countered with a knife-hand block. Against a bo thrust to the same area, the defender uses the right handle of the nunchaku to parry the blow. Front view at left.

DOWNWARD CROSS BLOCK

Without a weapon, a front kick is stopped by a downward cross block. Against a bo thrust to the same area, the defender crosses the nunchaku handles and uses the cord to block the bo. Front view at right.

FRONT VIEW

HIGH KNIFE-HAND BLOCK

Without a weapon, a punch to the face is countered with a high knife-hand block. Against a bo thrust to the same area, the defender uses the left handle of the nunchaku to deflect the strike. Front view at left.

FOREARM BLOCK

Attacked with a punch to the chest or neck, the karateka counters with a forearm block. Against a bo thrust to the same area, the defender uses the forward handle of the nunchaku, tilted outward in his left hand, to deflect the strike to the side. Front view at right.

STOMACH PUNCH

The nunchaku is driven directly into the opponent's midsection, in the same manner as the karate reverse punch. Front view at left.

ELBOW STRIKE

The nunchaku, held tightly along the right forearm, is driven upward into the opponent's chin, in the same mannner as the karate elbow strike. Front view at right.

FRONT VIEW

BACKHAND BLOW

The nunchaku is used to strike to the opponent's face, almost in the same manner as the karate back-knuckle strike. Front view at left.

DOUBLE PUNCH

The two nunchaku handles are driven into the opponent's stomach, in the same manner as the karate double punch. Front view at right.

FRONT VIEW

TIGER CLAW ATTACK

The string end of the nunchaku is driven to the opponent's throat, in the same manner as the karate tiger claw attack. Care must be taken to grip the nunchaku firmly in both hands. Front view at left.

CHOP

The nunchaku is swung to the opponent's neck or head in the same circular arc followed by the right-hand shuto in karate. This technique is illustrative of the nunchaku's superior range. Front view at right.

SPEAR-HAND ATTACK
The nunchaku handles are driven downward into the opponent's eyes, in the same manner as the karate spear-hand attack. Front view at left.

69

BASIC WHIPPING TECHNIQUES

Each movement of the nunchaku can be useful if serious thought is given to it. Simply throwing the nunchaku is easy, but using it in combat is very difficult. The snapping out and catching motions must be fast, and you must think ahead for your next move.

The swinging movement of the arm is the heart of the nunchaku. However, if you make a mistake, lose your balance, miss your grip, or leave yourself open to attack, you may lose a fight. With one swing, the nunchaku will double in size and shorten the distance between you and your opponent. It is best to wait until your opponent is fairly close to you to strike so he will not be warned of the unusually long range of the nunchaku.

The whipping motion of the nunchaku can be a very powerful movement. However, if your body and the weapon are not in balance, or if your timing is off, your efforts may be ineffective. Remember: With most whipping techniques, you must return to your original position.

Once you have mastered the basic nunchaku movements, practice blindfolded or in a dark room to acquire the feeling of circular movement, hand positions and timing.

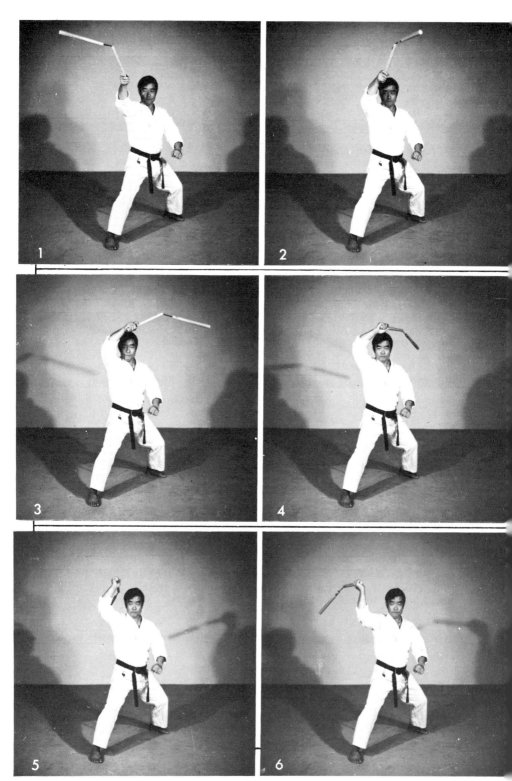

APPLICATION

OVERHEAD CIRCLE (Heiko-Kaiten)

Swing the nunchaku overhead in a circular whipping motion. Use a strong wrist action and practice swinging in both directions, first in small, then in larger circles. Use both high and low stances, and practice swinging while advancing, retreating and pivoting. Keep the rope taut enough to prevent the nunchaku from dropping. If you miss your opponent on the first strike, the overhand circle whip will provide a quick follow-up.

73

APPLICATION

CIRCULAR SIDE SWING (Yoko-Kaiten)

Swing the nunchaku at your side, keeping your right elbow close to your body and using wrist action to keep the nunchaku swinging in short circles. Practice swinging overhand and underhand from your left and right sides, gradually expanding the circumference of the circles.

APPLICATION

FIGURE EIGHT SWING (Hachiji-Gaeshi)

Swing the nunchaku in front of you in a figure eight from top right to bottom left. Keep the point at which the nunchaku crosses in front of you no lower than your shoulder and no higher than your ear. The greatest power is generated in the downward swing building into the figure eight. Keep the rope taut to avoid being whiplashed. Practice swinging while advancing, retreating and pivoting, and occasionally reverse the figure eight. This swing is especially effective against an opponent who weaves or ducks away from you.

3

6

CHANGING GRIP
(Kote-Gaeshi)

(1) Hold the nunchaku in both hands, (2) releasing the left hand and (3) allowing one handle to flip straight out. Manipulate the handle with your right hand so it swings back over the top, and (4) catch it with your left hand. (6) Repeat the action by releasing your *right* hand this time and manipulating the handle with your left hand, swinging it back over until (9) you catch it with your right hand. This hand change is fundamental to all nunchaku switches and should be practiced repeatedly so that your opponent will never know from which side to expect your attack.

9

10

ONE-HAND CHANGING GRIP
(Katate-Kote-Gaeshi)

(1) Grip both nunchaku handles in your right hand, placing the index finger between the handles. (2-4) Release the bottom handle and swing it up and over. (5) Just before recovering the released handle, change your grip to release the other handle. Repeat this technique often to help you recover the nunchaku quickly after making a pass.

APPLICATION

CROSS SWING AND CHANGE (Suihei-Gaeshi)

(1) Grip the handles of the fully-extended nunchaku overhead, (2) then release your right hand, (3) swinging the nunchaku in a complete circle in front of you, and (5) catching it with your right hand. Keep your motion smooth and rhythmic; don't leave yourself exposed by swinging too deeply. Practice changing from hand to hand and varying the angle of your swing.

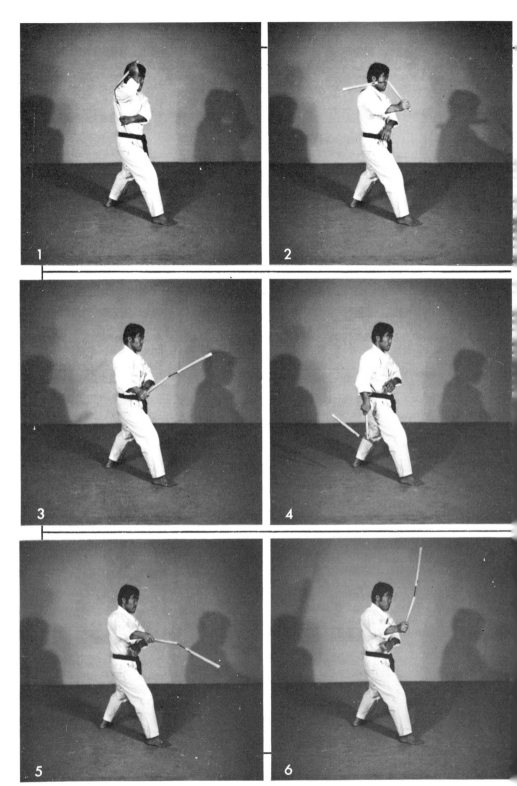

APPLICATION

REVERSE SHOULDER SWING (Kata-Sukashi)

(1) Place the nunchaku over the right shoulder, holding the top handle with your right hand and the lower with your left. (2) Swing it over your shoulder by snapping your right hand downward. (4) After completion of the swing, recover the nunchaku by returning it to your shoulder. Let the rope break the impact during recovery by looping it tight against your shoulder as you catch the nunchaku.

7

8

APPLICATION

UNDERARM GRIP (Waki-Basami)

(1) Place one handle of the nunchaku tightly under your right armpit, and grasp the other handle with your right hand. (2 & 3) Release the handle under your armpit with a sharp snap of the wrist. Your right elbow must be flared out for recovery, (7 & 8) permitting the nunchaku to be clamped under the armpit.

APPLICATION

UNDERHAND GRIP (Gyakute-Gaeshi)

(1) Place the nunchaku in front of your body, holding the upper handle in your right hand with a reverse grip (thumb near the edge) and the lower handle in your left in a natural position. (2-7) Release your left hand, using wrist action to swing the nunchaku into a figure eight. The nunchaku has its greatest impact on its downward path. (8) At the completion of the figure eight movement, recover the nunchaku with your left hand so that it is at its original position.

7

8

CROSS BACK SWING
(Fudo-Gaeshi)

(1) From the cross (diagonal) back position (close-up at left), (2) release the nunchaku with your left hand and (3-8) swing it out into a counterclockwise circle in front of you. Complete the initial swing by (9) letting the nun-

(CONTINUED ON PAGE 92)

Caution: Soften the impact of the nunchaku on recovery by looping the rope tightly around your hip or against your shoulder. Improper recovery of the nunchaku may result in painful injury.

(CONTINUED)

APPLICATION

chaku wrap around your left hip. (10-13) Then reverse your swing upward and (14) recover the nunchaku with your left hand behind you. Practice changing hands and swinging in circles and figure eights.

APPLICATION

DOUBLE NUNCHAKU TECHNIQUE (Morote-Furi)

The simultaneous use of two sets of nunchaku allows you to double your striking force. Use the two sets in the same manner as a single set—in circles, crosses and figure eights. Rely primarily on the underarm catch as a preparation or recovery technique when working with two sets.

5

6

9

10

FOOTWORK WITH
WHIPPING TECHNIQUES

Each technique must be practiced in all directions—forward, backward and to both sides—to develop balance, accurate footwork and rotating techniques. Combine different movements until the combinations are fast and smooth. When you practice for speed, however, be careful not to sacrifice the accuracy of your movements. You may have to try different stances with hand movements since stances that are strong and balanced in single movements may not be as effective in combination.

Everyone knows that for a beginner good technique comes from good form. Often, students of the nunchaku try to move on to the next technique before finishing the preceding movement. Do not forget that the ideal movement is perfect in form and places you in a balanced position for the next move.

CROSS SWING AND CHANGE
(Suihei-Gaeshi)

Footwork is primarily practiced to develop hip power. (3) Step forward with your forward (left) foot, (4 & 5) simultaneously whipping your hips and completing your cross swing of the nunchaku. (6) Recover the nunchaku overhead and (8) cross swing with your left hand. (9) Always concentrate on attaining maximum power from your swing by whipping your hips into the movement.

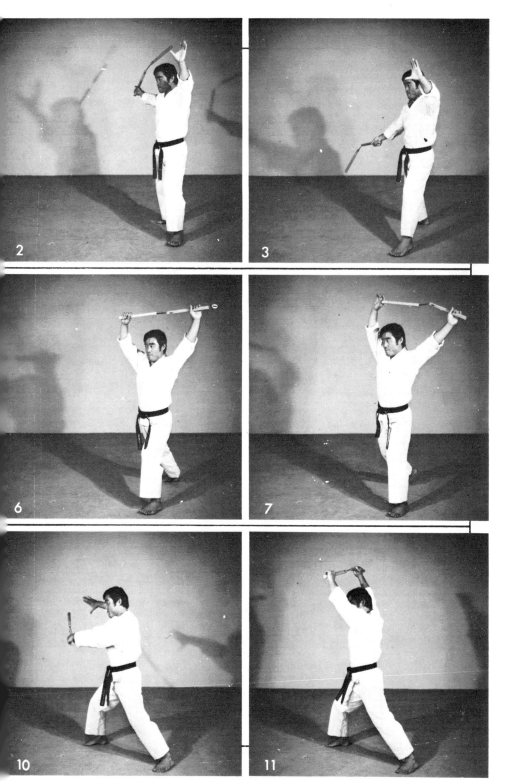

CROSS BACK SWING
(Fudo-Gaeshi)

Using the preceding exercise as a foundation, gradually begin to practice changing hands and alternating your swings while advancing or retreating, as illustrated here. Always concentrate on whipping your hips while swinging.

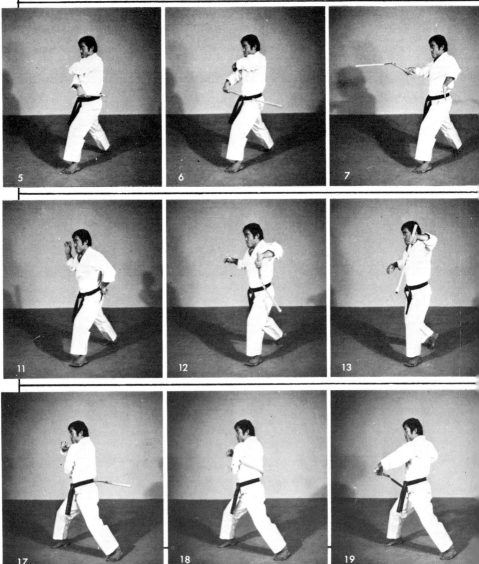

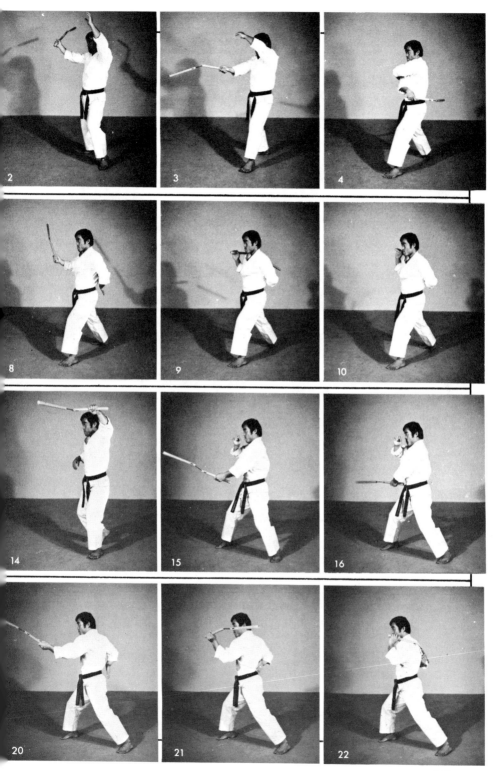

APPLIED ATTACKING TECHNIQUES

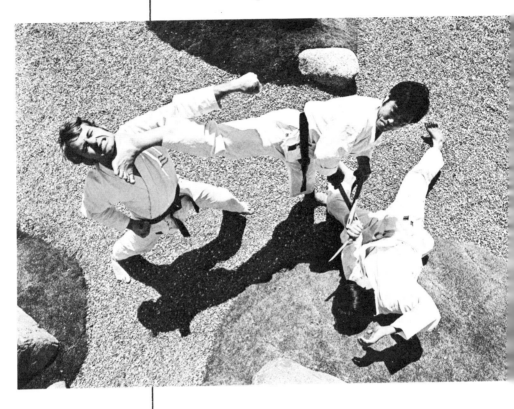

CAUTION: The sparring techniques simulated here are for instruction only. Students should never attempt live sparring against an opponent.

OVERHAND STRIKE

Hold both handles of the nunchaku in a prepared position overhead, then release one handle with the left hand and swing the nunchaku overhand to your opponent's head, collarbone or arms.

SIDE POSITION STRIKE

Hold both handles of the nunchaku in a prepared position on your left hip, then release one handle with your rear (left) hand and swing the nunchaku backhand to your opponent's head, ribs or knees.

CROSS BACK STRIKE
(from behind)

Hold the nunchaku diagonally behind your back, grasping one handle with your right hand over your right shoulder and the other handle with your left hand at your waist. Release one handle with either hand and swing the nunchaku to your opponent's chin, groin, arm or knee.

VARIATION OF
HIDDEN HAND TECHNIQUE
(from behind)

(1) Wrap the nunchaku around your back so your opponent won't know from which side to expect your attack. (2-5) Release the left handle of the nunchaku and swing with your right hand in a circular motion to your opponent's knee, then (7) loop a reverse swing above your head, (10) striking downward to your opponent's head in a smooth, continuous motion.

DRAWING ATTACK TECHNIQUE

The nunchaku is most easily drawn from your belt when the unattached ends stick upward (rope down) so that you can grasp the upper handles and (3-6) strike to your opponent's head in the same motion. You can then (9 & 10) loop a reverse swing above your head in a circle or figure eight and (11) strike downward again to your opponent's head in a smooth, continuous motion.

UNDERARM GRIP TECHNIQUE

(1) Place one nunchaku handle under your right armpit and grasp the other handle with your forward (right) hand. (2-4) Release the handle under your armpit with a sharp snap of your wrist to (5) hit your opponent's head, collarbone or arm.

APPLIED BLOCK AND COUNTER TECHNIQUES

SWEEP BLOCK AND COUNTER

To defend against a punch to the face or chest, (2) take a step backward and (3) parry the blow with the nunchaku handle. (4) Draw the upper handle back in a continued motion and (5-6) counter to your opponent's head.

SWINGING BLOCK
AND COUNTER

To defend against a low attack with a bo, (2) place the nunchaku in front of you and prepare to block by (3) raising the weapon overhead. (4) Release the nunchaku with your left hand and (5) snap your wrist downward to make the block. (6-9) Follow up by swinging the nunchaku overhead in a continuous motion and striking downward to your opponent's head.

COMBINATION THRUST BLOCK WITH A ROUNDHOUSE KICK

(1 & 2) To defend against a high attack with or without a weapon, hold the nunchaku in front of you. (3) Take a step back and meet the attack with (5) an upward block, at the same time positioning yourself in a strong forward stance. After stopping the blow, (8) counter with a roundhouse kick to the chin or neck.

COMBINATION THRUST BLOCK WITH A FRONT SNAP KICK

(1) To defend against a high attack with or without a weapon, hold the nunchaku in front of you. (3) Move into a cat stance and (4) meet the opponent's attack with an upward block. (5) Then quickly counter with a (6) front snap kick, followed by a (9) nunchaku jab to the eyes, throat and stomach.

2

3

5

6

8

9

JAMMING BLOCK ATTACK

To defend against an attack to your body, (1) hold both nunchaku handles horizontally in front of you and (2) step in to meet your opponent's attack. (3) Jam the nunchaku into your opponent's arm and body, and (5) follow up with an attack to his chin or face.

THRUSTING BLOCK DOWNWARD

To defend against a front kick, (2 & 3) thrust the nunchaku downward and block the kick with the rope. (5) Quickly counter with the nunchaku to your opponent's face or stomach.

SWEEP BLOCK VARIATION

To defend against a high attack with or without a weapon, (4) parry the attack with the nunchaku. (5) Reach back for leverage, then (7) counter with a strike to the face, stomach or chest with the butt of the right handle.

2

4

5

7

PINCH BLOCK

(1) To defend against an attack to your face or midsection, hold the nunchaku in front of you. (3) Step back and block with the fully extended nunchaku. Then (4) loop the opponent's wrist with the nunchaku rope and pinch, (5-7) jerking your opponent to the ground. (8 & 9) Finish with a stomp to the body.

ARM AND NUNCHAKU COMBINATION BLOCK

To defend against a side kick, (2) sidestep the attack and (4) block with your right forearm. If your opponent follows up with a backhand strike, (5) block it with the nunchaku and (7) proceed to choke him from behind.

INSIDE SWEEP BLOCK

To defend against a high attack with or without a weapon, (2) take a step backward and (3) parry the attack with the nunchaku, quickly moving toward the opponent. (4) Raise the weapon high so that you can loop the opponent's head with the rope and (5) apply a choke from the front. Then, (7) pull your opponent toward you and drive your knee into his groin or solar plexus.

2

4

5

7

UPWARD NUNCHAKU BLOCK

(1) To defend against a high attack with or without a weapon, retreat by stepping back with your left foot, (4 & 5) keeping the nunchaku in front of you for protection. Just before being hit, (6) block with an upward motion. At this point, your opponent is vulnerable to any counters below his arms. (7) Immediately release the nunchaku with your left hand, (8) looping it over your head and (9 & 10) swinging it down into the opponent's ribs.

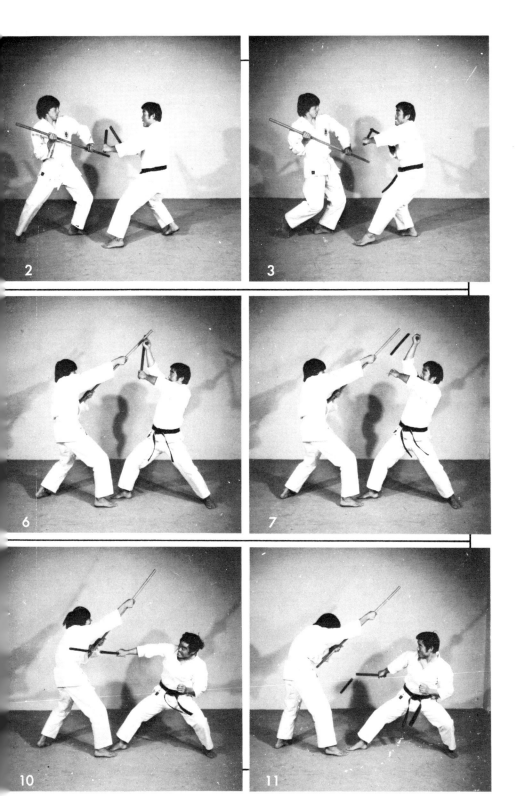

UPWARD CROSS BLOCK

To defend against a high attack with a *bo* (staff), (3) retreat with your right foot and (4 & 5) thrust your nunchaku upward into a cross block. (7) Release one end of the nunchaku and (8 & 9) swing it in a smooth circle (10 & 11) to the groin area. Note: Your left hand should be raised high to protect your head.

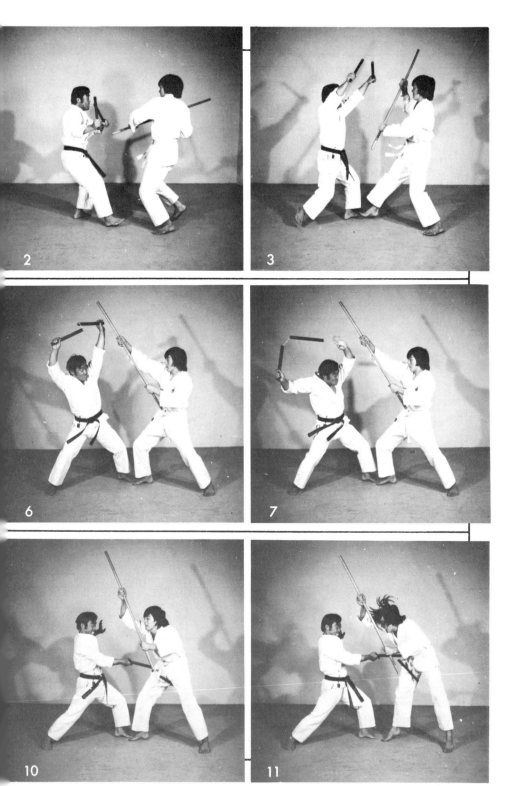

JUMP DEFENSE

To defend against an attack to (5 & 6) your lower legs, it is often more effective to jump over, rather than block, the blow. Begin swinging the nunchaku (7) as you leap, and (10) strike your opponent while you are still in mid-air, before he has completed his attack. (11) It will then be possible to continue striking when you land.

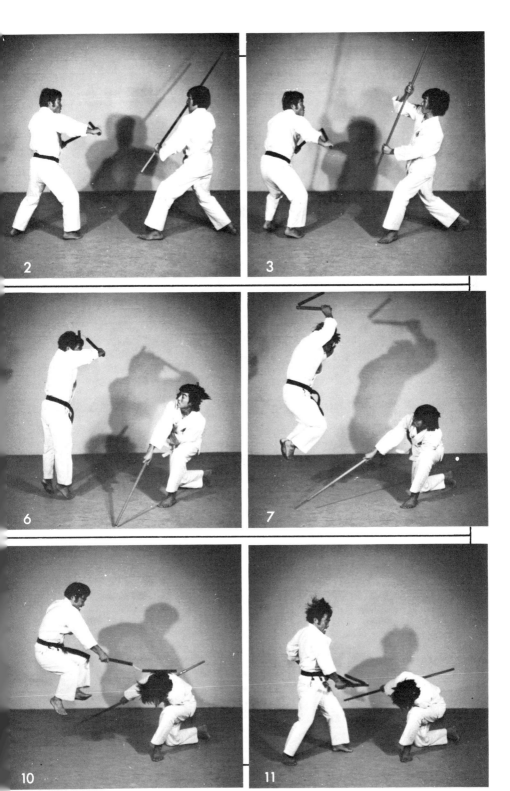

ATTACK, COUNTERED, ATTACK AGAIN

When an opponent (3 & 4) evades your initial attack, the flexibility of the nunchaku makes it possible for you to still strike on the counterswing. Recover the nunchaku by (5) letting it wrap around your body. Then reverse your swing and (8) strike to the inside of your opponent's knee, all in a smooth, continuous motion.

PINCH BLOCK

To defend against a front spearing attack with a weapon or a lunge punch, use the nunchaku to (3) seize the weapon or arm and (4 & 5) jerk it sharply away from your opponent. (6) As soon as the opponent's weapon has been dislodged, counterattack with a basic backhand swing (10) to the kidneys, knees or head.

2

3

6

7

10

11

FOREARM BLOCK AND NUNCHAKU COUNTER

To defend against a side kick, your best counter may be to combine a karate block with a nunchaku strike. Stop your opponent's kick by (4) stepping back with your right foot and (5) blocking with your left forearm. Counter by swinging the nunchaku (11) to your opponent's groin or across the back of his head.

2

3

6

7

10

11

139

SACRIFICE COUNTERATTACK

To defend against an opponent who (5) successfully sweeps your left foot, (6) pivot completely to the right on your right foot, and swing your nunchaku while dropping to one knee. (7) Bring your opponent down with a counterswing to the back of his knee, and (10) follow up with an overhand strike to his head. Note: In situations like this, the length of the nunchaku permits you to be unbalanced and to give ground without conceding control to your opponent.

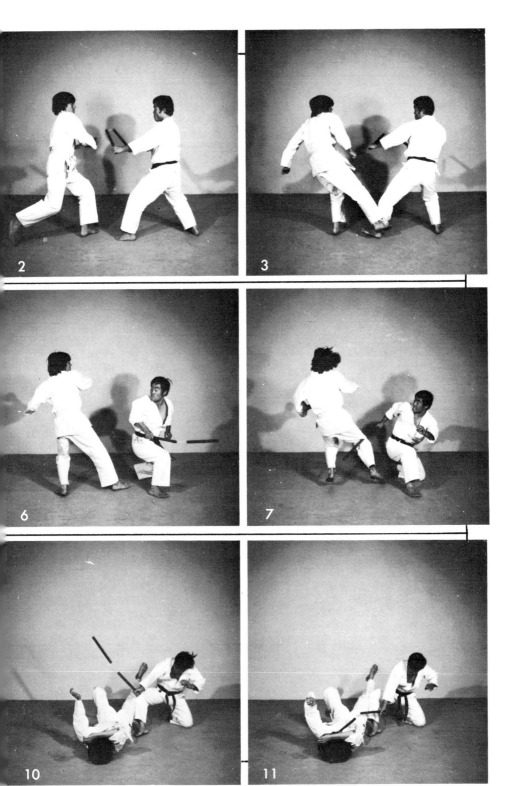

DOUBLE NUNCHAKU BLOCK

To defend against a high attack with or without a weapon, (3) take a step back with your right foot and (4) block the opponent's attack with one set of nunchaku, (5-8) countering to his kidneys with the second set. (10) Strike again with the nunchaku that was used to block.

BLACK BELT™ VIDEO PRESENTS

NUNCHAKU: KARATE WEAPON OF SELF-DEFENSE
By Fumio Demura
Students are taught to use the *nunchaku* in a traditional manner. Topics covered: how to grip, stances, blocking, striking, calisthenics, karate and nunchaku similarities, and whipping, applied attacking, and applied block and counter.
Code No. 1010-VHS (60 min.)

BRUCE LEE'S FIGHTING METHOD: Basic Training and Self-Defense Techniques
By Ted Wong and Richard Bustillo
Bruce Lee's *jeet kune do*, as explained in *Bruce Lee's Fighting Method*. This covers the first two volumes, with topics including warm-ups, basic exercises, on-guard position, footwork, power/speed training and self-defense.
Code No. 1020-VHS (55 min.)

TAI CHI CHUAN
By Marshall Ho'o
World expert in *tai chi chuan* teaches this Chinese practice, which promotes mind-body awareness and rejuvenation. Topics covered: the nine temple exercises, the short form, push hands and self-defense applications.
Code No. 1030-VHS (90 min.)

KARATE (SHITO-RYU)
By Fumio Demura
This program includes: warm-up exercises; an analysis of basics, including striking points, target areas, standing positions, and hand, elbow, kicking and blocking techniques; three ten-minute workouts; and a demo of basic sparring and self-defense.
Code No. 1040-VHS (90 min.)

Rainbow Publications Inc.
Mail to:
Black Belt Magazine Video
P.O. Box 918, Santa Clarita, California 91380-9018
Or Call:
Toll-Free 1(800)423-2874